Jellyfish and Octopuses

Elsie Nelley

Contents

Sea Creatures without Bones 2

Jellyfish Bodies 8

Octopus Bodies 10

Food for Jellyfish 14

Food for Octopuses 16

Dangers for Jellyfish and Octopuses 18

A Dangerous Jellyfish 20

A Dangerous Octopus 22

Amazing Sea Creatures 23

Glossary and Index 24

Sea Creatures without Bones

Jellyfish and octopuses are sea creatures.

They have been living in oceans on Earth for more than 600 million years.

Jellyfish and octopuses have soft bodies. They are not fish, because they have no bones.

A Spotted Jellyfish moves through the sea.

An octopus swims underwater.

Jellyfish can swim, but most of the time,
they drift and float with the ocean tides.
The movement of waves pushes and pulls them into groups.

A large group of jellyfish is called a "bloom."
Sometimes, a group is also called a "swarm" or a "smack."

Think and Talk About ...
Winds sometimes blow
thousands of jellyfish
onto beaches.

Jellyfish drift together
in a group or "bloom."

Octopuses can swim fast, but only for short distances.
Most of the time, they crawl along the ocean floor.

Octopuses live alone near the bottom of the ocean.
During the day, they hide in **crevices**, under rocks,
or inside holes they have dug.
They come out to feed when it is dark.

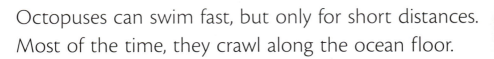

An octopus comes out of its hole
to feed at night.

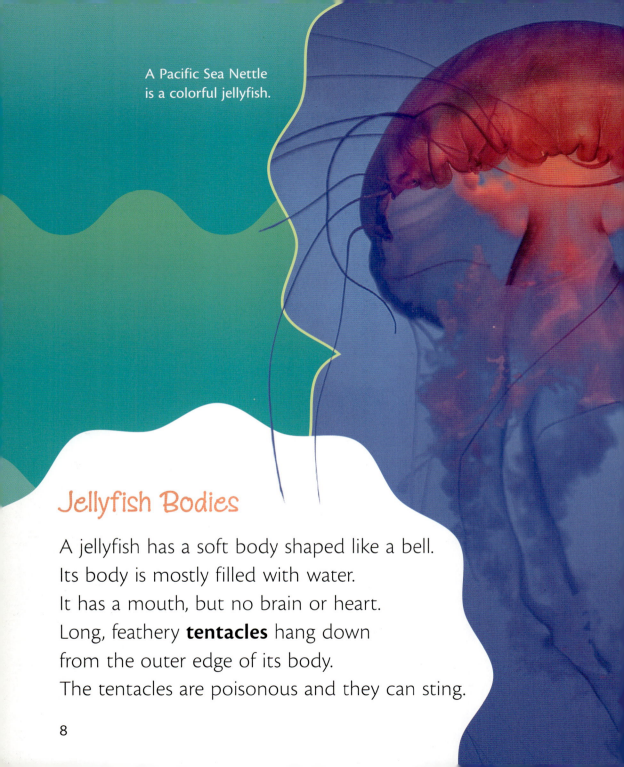

A Pacific Sea Nettle
is a colorful jellyfish.

Jellyfish Bodies

A jellyfish has a soft body shaped like a bell.
Its body is mostly filled with water.
It has a mouth, but no brain or heart.
Long, feathery **tentacles** hang down
from the outer edge of its body.
The tentacles are poisonous and they can sting.

8

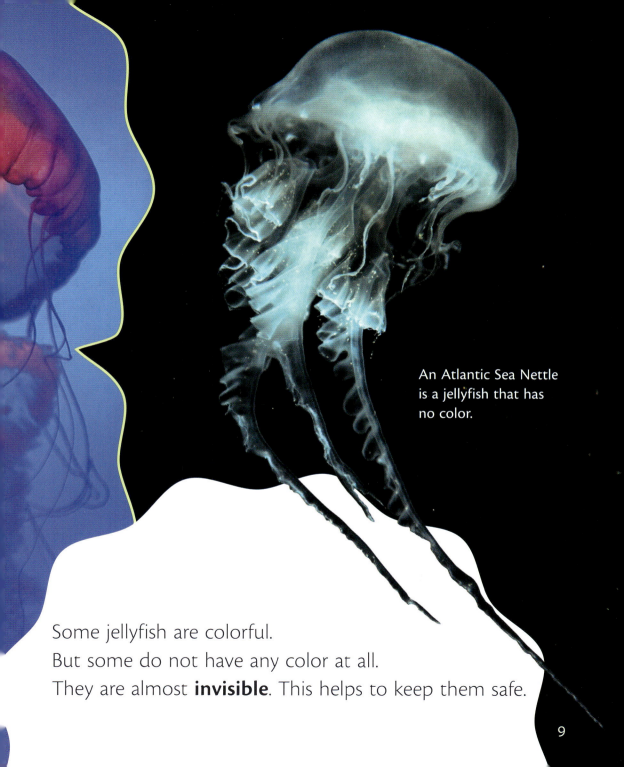

An Atlantic Sea Nettle is a jellyfish that has no color.

Some jellyfish are colorful.
But some do not have any color at all.
They are almost **invisible**. This helps to keep them safe.

Octopus Bodies

An octopus is often a reddish-brown color.
It has a large head and eight long arms.
Its arms are joined to its head.
Each arm is covered with two rows of round suckers.

An octopus uses its long arms and suckers to catch food,
and to move across the ocean floor.

The biggest octopus in the world is the Giant Pacific Octopus.
It can have as many as 280 suckers down each arm.

Think and Talk About ...

Octopus is a Greek word
meaning "eight feet."

A Giant Pacific Octopus crawls along the ocean floor.

An octopus has a brain, two big eyes, and three hearts.

If an octopus is attacked, it can hide
by changing its color and shape.
It will often make itself look like a shell,
a rock, or even a plant.

An octopus that loses an arm can grow another one!

An octopus hides
in a coral reef.

Food for Jellyfish

Jellyfish do not have to hunt for their food,
because everything they eat is all around them in the ocean.

A Moon Jellyfish swims
among corals
and small fish.

They feed on small sea animals, fish eggs, and sea snails that get trapped in their long tentacles.

Jellyfish eat other jellyfish, too.

A Bluefire Jellyfish has a fish caught in its tentacles.

Food for Octopuses

Octopuses move quietly through the water
when searching for crabs and shellfish.
They are greedy hunters and will squeeze their soft bodies
through tiny spaces to trap their prey.

An octopus uses its strong arms and suckers
to open the hard shell of a sea animal.
It has a sharp beak hidden inside its mouth.
Sometimes, it uses its sharp beak to drill holes in the shell.
Then, it sucks out the soft parts from inside the shell.

Octopuses are very clever animals.

Think and Talk About ...

It is difficult to keep an octopus
in a tank. It needs a lot of space
and it will try to escape!

An octopus eats a sea animal.
The octopus's mouth is
underneath its body.

Dangers for Jellyfish and Octopuses

Jellyfish are hunted by large fish and sea turtles.
Some sea turtles can chew only soft food,
so jellyfish are good for them to eat.

A Hawksbill Sea Turtle
eats a jellyfish.

Octopuses are hunted by large fish and sharks.

But an octopus is able to frighten its attacker.
It sprays a cloud of black ink into the water.
While the water is dark and cloudy, the octopus **escapes**.

A Giant Pacific Octopus sprays ink and swims away.

Think and Talk About ...

Sea turtles sometimes swallow plastic bags in the water because they look like jellyfish.

A Dangerous Jellyfish

The Box Jellyfish is the most dangerous jellyfish in the world.
It has tentacles as long as ten feet.
They hang down from the sides of its body.

Box Jellyfish can have tentacles ten feet long!

A sting from one of these tentacles is very poisonous. A person who gets stung must be taken to a doctor or a hospital straight away.

At some beaches in Australia, there are bright-yellow signs to warn people about the dangers of Box Jellyfish.

Think and Talk About ...

Long nets that catch jellyfish are put on some beaches to make them safer for swimmers.

A sign warns people about Box Jellyfish at a beach in Western Australia.

STINGERS

A Dangerous Octopus

The tiny Blue-Ringed Octopus is found in rock pools around the coast of Australia.
It is only about the size of a golf ball.

When the octopus gets upset, it turns yellow, and shiny blue rings **appear** all over its body.

The Blue-Ringed Octopus has a very poisonous bite!
It is one of the most deadly creatures in the ocean.

Blue-Ringed Octopuses live in rock pools.

Amazing Sea Creatures

Jellyfish and octopuses
are found in oceans all around the world.

Although they can sting or bite,
only a few jellyfish and octopuses are **harmful** to people.

Jellyfish and octopuses are amazing sea creatures.

A sting from the
Pacific Sea Nettle
is not usually harmful.

The Common Octopus
is a clever sea animal.

Glossary

appear (*verb*) to be seen or become visible

crevices (*noun*) narrow cracks in rocks or walls

escapes (*verb*) flees or gets away

harmful (*adjective*) dangerous

invisible (*adjective*) not able to be seen

tentacles (*noun*) long, thin arms on some creatures

Index

Blue-Ringed Octopus 22

bodies 8–13

Box Jellyfish 20–21

color 9

danger 18–22

food 14–18

Giant Pacific Octopus 10–11, 19

jellyfish 2, 4–5, 8–9, 14–15

oceans 2, 4, 6, 14, 23

octopuses 2–3, 6–7, 10–13, 16–17

sea turtles 18–19

tentacles 8, 15, 20, 21